BEEP BEEP, VROOM VROOM!

by Stuart J. Murphy • illustrated by Chris Demarest

HarperCollinsPublishers

LEVEL
1

To Kristin and Arnie—
with a kiss kiss
and a hug hug
to a great future together
—S.J.M.

For Ethan
—C.D.

The publisher and author would like to thank teachers Patricia Chase, Phyllis Goldman,
and Pat Hopfensperger for their help in making the math in MathStart just right for kids.

HarperCollins®, 📖®, and MathStart® are registered trademarks of HarperCollins Publishers.
For more information about the MathStart series, write to HarperCollins Children's Books,
10 East 53rd Street, New York, NY 10022.

Bugs incorporated in the MathStart series were painted by Jon Buller.

Beep-Beep, Vroom-Vroom!
Text copyright © 2000 by Stuart J. Murphy

Library of Congress Cataloging in Publication Data
Murphy, Stuart J., 1942–
    Beep beep, vroom vroom! / by Stuart Murphy ; illustrated by Chris Demarest.
        p.   cm. — (MathStart)
    "Level 1, Patterns."
    ISBN 0-06-028016-6. — ISBN 0-06-446728-7 (pbk.) — ISBN 0-06-028017-4 (lib. bdg.)
    1. Sequences (Mathematics)—Juvenile literature.   2. Automobiles—Juvenile literature.
I. Demarest, Chris L., ill.   II. Title.   III. Series.
QA246.5.M87   2000   98-51907
515'.24—DC21   CIP
                                                                                              AC

Typography by Elynn Cohen
8   9   10
❖
First Edition

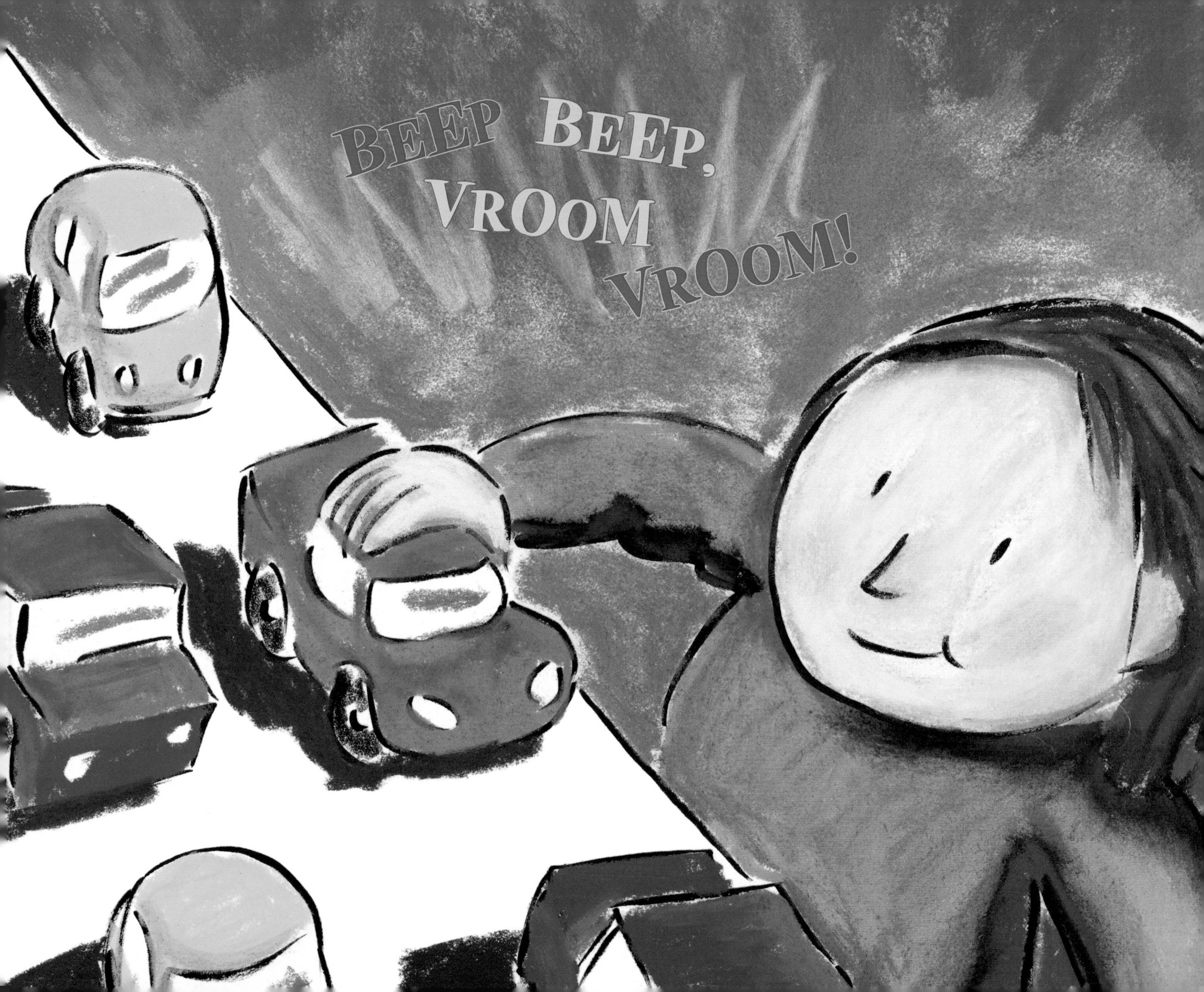
BEEP BEEP,
VROOM
VROOM!

BEEP BEEP honked the yellow cars.

VROOM VROOM zoomed the red cars.

4

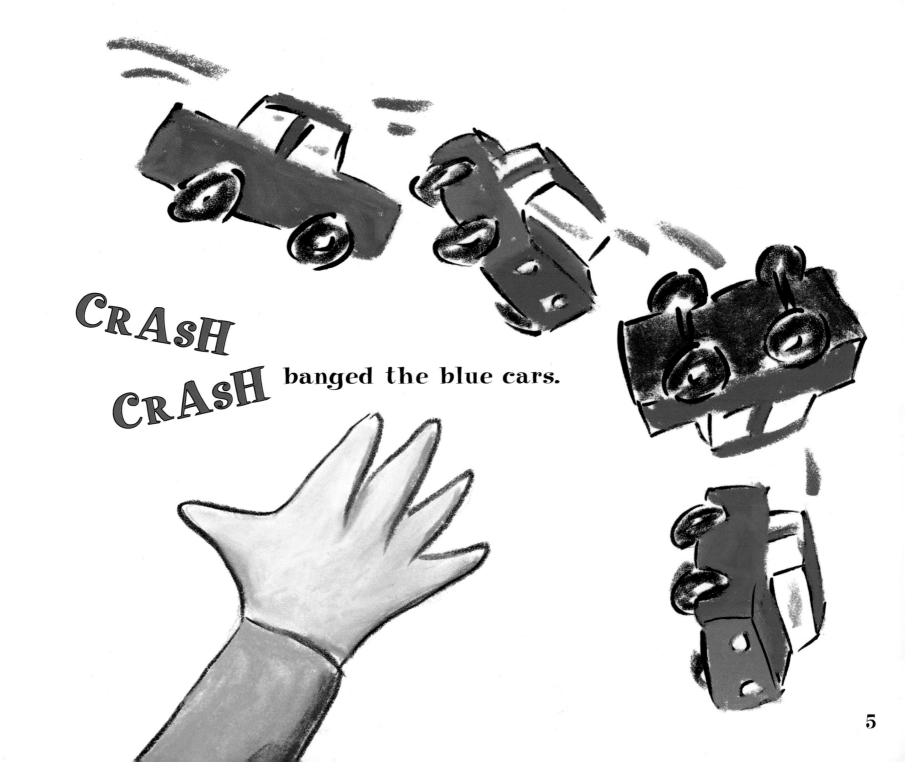

CRASH
CRASH banged the blue cars.

"Cars are fun," said Kevin, "for big kids to play with."

"I like cars," said Molly.

"You're too little to play with *my* cars," said Kevin.

7

"Kevin," called Mom. "It's your turn to set the table."
"Aww, Mom," grumbled Kevin. He carefully lined up
all the cars on his shelf.

"When I come back," Kevin told Molly, "I want to see my cars just the way I left them."

Molly waited until Kevin went downstairs.
Then . . .

VrOoM
VrOoM zoomed the red cars.

BeEp
BeEp honked the yellow cars.

10

CRASH CRASH banged the blue cars.

Dad heard lots of vrooming, crashing, and beeping.

"Molly," Dad said, "you know you shouldn't play with Kevin's cars unless you ask. Let's put them right back where you found them. Kevin always lines his cars up a special way."

Molly waited until Dad went downstairs.

Then . . .

CRASH
CRASH

banged the blue cars.

BEEP BEEP honked the yellow cars.

VROOM VROOM zoomed the red cars.

This time Mom heard all the crashing, beeping, and vrooming.

"Oh, Molly," Mom said. "You've made a big mess of Kevin's cars. Can you help me put them back the way he lines them up?"

17

Molly waited until Mom went downstairs.

Then . . .

BEEP BEEP honked the yellow cars.

VROOM
VROOM
zoomed the red cars.

CRASH
CRASH

banged the blue cars.

Now Digger heard the beeping,
vrooming, and crashing.
"Woof," Digger barked. "Woof, woof!"
Digger gave Molly lots of kisses. And
he wagged his tail—a little too much.

"Molly!" called Kevin from the kitchen. "You'd better not be playing with my cars! I'm coming upstairs to see!"

23

Molly put the cars back on the shelf as fast
as she could.

She could hear Kevin coming closer and closer.
Molly looked at the cars. They didn't look quite
right. She lined them up again quickly.

When Kevin walked in the door, he found
his cars . . . just the way he left them.

VrOoM VrOoM zoomed the red cars.

BeEp BeEp honked the yellow cars.

CrAsH CrAsH banged the blue cars.

"Maybe someday you'll be old enough to play with cars too, Molly," said Kevin.

"Surprise, Molly!" said Mom. She was standing in
the doorway. "We were going to wait until your
birthday to give you these, but we think you're old
enough to have them now."

Molly smiled at the shiny new cars.

Then . . .

BEEP honked the green cars.
BEEP

VROOM zoomed the purple cars.
VROOM

CRASH!

31

In *Beep Beep, Vroom Vroom!* the math concept is arranging objects in a definite and predictable pattern. Recognizing and extending patterns is important in the development of logical thinking.

If you would like to have more fun with the math concepts presented in *Beep Beep, Vroom Vroom!*, here are a few suggestions.

- Read the story with the child and ask him or her to describe the patterns in which Molly places the cars on the shelf. The child might describe the pattern by color or by type of car.

- Reread the story and have the child show the different patterns using toy cars or colored blocks.

- There are several patterns in the story that use the colors and shapes of the cars. Can you find a pattern with the sounds the cars make as well?

- Have the child arrange stuffed animals, dolls, or other toys on his or her bed in different patterns. Keep count of how many different ways they can be arranged (for example, "big, small, big").

- Arrange coins in a pattern (for example, "penny, penny, nickel, penny, penny, nickel" or "PPN PPN"). Ask the child, "Can you figure out what comes next?" Help the child continue the pattern, using extra coins. Patterns that you may wish to try: PPN PPN or PNP PNP or PPNN PPNN.

Following are some activities that will help you extend the concepts presented in *Beep Beep, Vroom Vroom!* into a child's everyday life.

In the Kitchen: Create a pattern with knives, forks, and spoons. Have the child first describe the pattern to you and then extend it with one or two repetitions.

Pattern Game: Collect pebbles or other small objects. The first player creates a pattern (such as "1 pebble, 2 pebbles, 1 pebble, 3 pebbles") and the second player must try to continue it. Then the second player creates a pattern for the first player to continue.

Button Pattern: Using buttons or other small objects, arrange them in the following pattern: 2 buttons, 4 buttons, 6 buttons, etc. Ask the child if he or she can continue the pattern. Help the child understand that even though the pattern never repeats, it can still be predicted because each group of buttons has two more than the previous group.

The following books include some of the same concepts that are presented in *Beep Beep, Vroom Vroom!*:

- THE BUTTON BOX by Margarette S. Reid

- CAPS FOR SALE by Esphyr Slobodkina

- NATURE'S PAINTBRUSH: *The Patterns and Colors Around You* by Susan Stockdale